THE LITTLE LAMB

Meets Lonely

Written By: Patrick McCullough
Illustrated By: Denise Armstrong

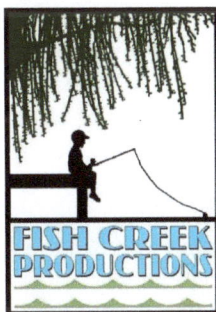

FISH CREEK PRODUCTIONS, LLC.
P. O. Box 131401
Spring, TX. 77393

832.341.2372

ISBN 13: 978-0-9973651-3-9
ISBN 10: 0-9973651-3-7

Library of Congress Control Number: 2017949004

ACKNOWLEDGMENTS

I would like to thank my many friends who have supported me in this process. I would also like to thank Denise Armstrong for her beautiful illustrations that make the text come alive. Lastly, and most importantly, I wish to thank my wife for her support and love to make my dream come true.

DEDICATION

I dedicate this book to all the children who
have lost a friend.

This is a story
of a little lamb named Lonely
who has lost her best friend.

As Pure-in-Heart and Curious continue their journey to seek a new pasture for the Good Shepherd's flock, they approach a flock of sheep and lambs grazing on a hillside. As they approach, all the sheep and lambs run to them and gather around Pure-in-Heart and Curious.

Everyone is excited to see new friends. One of them asks where they were coming from. Pure-in-Heart says, "We left our home to go on a special mission for the Good Shepherd to find a new pasture for His flock."

Once Pure-in-Heart shared this, everyone became very happy and invited Pure-in-Heart and Curious to stay with them and share their experiences with the Good Shepherd. As Pure-in-Heart was speaking, Curious noticed one lamb standing by herself.

Curious walked up to the lamb and said, "Hello my name is Curious, what is your name?" The lamb said sadly, "My name is Lonely." Puzzled, Curious asked her, "Why are you called Lonely?"

"Mercy, my best friend in the whole world, has died." Curious felt so sorry for Lonely, for he knew that losing someone very close is hard to understand.

As Pure-in-Heart was sharing with everyone he saw Curious in the distance speaking with a lamb that was all by herself.

He came over and asked Curious, "Who is your new friend?" Curious said, "Her name is Lonely".

Pure-in-Heart then asked, "Why is she so sad?" Curious said "Because her best friend recently died."

Pure-in-Heart asked Lonely, "What happened to your friend?" Lonely shared, "One day we were having fun, playing with the other lambs, but the next day my friend, Mercy, did not show up to play."

"I did not think it was strange, because sometimes our parents have us do chores and run errands. The next day Mercy did not show up again and that is when I got worried. So, I went to see her to find out why she did not come out to play?"

"When I got there, my friend, Mercy, was lying on the grass and appeared like she was asleep, but her parents told me that she was very sick." Pure-in-Heart and Curious looked at each other feeling the pain of their new friend's sadness.

Pure-in-Heart asked, "Then what happened?" "I went back a few days later to visit Mercy and her parents told me that she was not getting any better and I could see Mercy looked so pale and weak.

I felt so sad that I wanted to give her something to cheer her up. When I went back the next day, I brought her favorite flowers that I picked especially for her and they made her smile.

When I went to see her a few days later to see how she was doing, her parents told me that she passed away the night before. I was so upset that I ran to a place where no one could see me and cried and cried. I just could not understand why my best friend died."

Pure-in-Heart and Curious felt so sad for Lonely after listening to her experience of losing her friend. As they were comforting her, suddenly, the Good Shepherd appeared. He stood there before the three lambs. He then knelt and stretched out his arms to hold Lonely.

Lonely closed her eyes and rested in the strong, comforting arms of the Good Shepherd. He then looked at Lonely and said, "I know you are very sad and feel alone. I understand how you feel and the pain you are experiencing my Little One."

"I was with your best friend, Mercy, during the time she was very sick. I never left her side. I told her not to be afraid, for I would be with her now and always."

"We laughed and talked about how much fun you two had together. She also told me that you were her best friend in the whole world, and that she loved you very much."

"I told Mercy that she would be going to a new place where she will always be healthy and will make new friends. Your best friend became very excited when I told her this."

"Mercy then looked up and said she could not go to this place without you for she knew once she was gone, you would be so sad and alone."

Suddenly, Lonely spoke up very excited, .
"I want to go to this place, too!" The
Good Shepherd said, "It is not your time
to go there. But, fear not My little
friend, I will always be with you. I will
be your Companion while Mercy is
gone."

Lonely looked up at the Good Shepherd and asked, "Where is this new place and when can I go there?" The Good Shepherd smiled and patted Lonely on her head. He said, "This new place is far away and it is a place for those whose time here has come to an end."

Lonely asked, "When will it be my time? I really want to be with my friend, Mercy." The Good Shepherd said, "No one knows when their time will come to leave. Sometimes it happens suddenly, sometimes it takes longer."

The Good Shepherd said, "Be comforted Lonely, for your best friend is always with you." Lonely looked up at the Good Shepherd confused, because she did not understand what He meant.

The Good Shepherd placed his hand on Lonely's chest, right over her heart, and said, "This is where your friend is. She will always be there for you. When you think of Mercy, your loneliness will go away and be replaced with joy and happiness."

"Now that you know this, your name will no longer be Lonely. Your new name will be Joyful". Joyful looked at the Good Shepherd, then to her two new friends and was so happy knowing she will not be lonely anymore.

The next day Joyful said goodbye to her two new friends as they continued their journey for the Good Shepherd.

Verse that relates to the story:

Ecclesiastes 3: 1, 2 and 4

A Time for Everything

3 ¹ There is a time for everything,
and a season for every activity under
the heavens:
² A time to be born and a time to die...,
⁴ A time to weep and a time to laugh,
a time to mourn and a time to
dance.

The Characteristics of the Butterfly in Scripture

The most spectacular characteristic of the butterfly is its transformation from caterpillar to butterfly. The monarch butterfly absorbs bitter toxins during its early development, which protects its life when it matures. Similarly, God allows harsh experiences in our youth.

10 And the God of all grace, who called you to his eternal glory in Christ, after you have suffered a little while, will himself restore you and make you strong, firm and steadfast. (1 Peter 5:10)

ABOUT THE AUTHOR

Patrick McCullough was born in Cleveland Ohio. In the early years of his life, he never stayed in one place very long because his Father was in the United States Coast Guard. After college, he had an opportunity to work in the oil and gas industry where he traveled throughout the world. In this profession, he had many opportunities to visit children in 3rd world countries. He was touched by their simplistic way of life which inspired him to reach out to the children and began telling them stories about God. This further lead Patrick to bring cases of children's books to the different countries he visited.

This book was written to help children relate to situations that may occur in their own lives while growing up and in a way to help them embrace the lesson, and understand the importance of the message. This story was inspired when he was asked to tell a story during a children's church school class. Not wanting to share the same old stories, he went to bed hoping that a story would come to his mind. When he woke up, God had given him this story to share.

Patrick currently lives in Houston, Texas with his wife and dog.

ABOUT THE ILLUSTRATOR

Denise Has been working in the fine arts for over 38 yrs. Upon earning a degree in Graphic Design, she first went to work in the advertising department of a local newspaper office. Since those early days her training has become progressive as many opportunities opened up for her to use a myriad of mediums. Some projects have ranged from sculptures, portraiture, pen and ink, illustrations to large scale canvas oils and murals. Ongoing she has exhibited in galleries both locally and internationally.
All of her creations are an expression of her soul, revealing what is imprinted on her heart.

Denise lives and studio's in Montgomery, Texas with her husband Jesse. They have two sons Luke, Matthew and daughter-in-law Kate. A daughter Emily, Son-in-Law-Eric and grand-daughter Vera.

www.denisearmstrong.com

www.ingramcontent.com/pod-product-compliance
Lightning Source LLC
Chambersburg PA
CBHW041426090426
42741CB00002B/47

* 9 7 8 0 9 9 7 3 6 5 1 3 9 *